HOUSTON

THE CITY AT A

CW00796793

Chase Tower
IM Pei's perfectly pro
skyscraper, complete
north end of the Dov
See p015

Pennzoil Place
With this arresting 1975 building, Johnson/
Burgee introduced Houston to the idea that
corporate architecture need not be dull.
See p066

One Shell Plaza
SOM's 1971 HQ for Shell Oil is an innovative
lightweight concrete structure featuring
distinctive ripples on its lower facade.
910 Louisiana Street

Wells Fargo Plaza
Edward C Bassett and Lawrence Doane of
SOM conceived this bank tower as two offset
quarter-circles sheathed in emerald glass.
1000 Louisiana Street

Heritage Plaza
Houston's 1980s construction boom ended
with this PoMo fantasy inspired by Mayan
ruins that architect Mohammed Nasr saw
while on holiday in Yucatán, Mexico.
1111 Bagby Street

1400 Smith Street
The former home of Enron, this elegant 1983
high-rise by Lloyd Jones Brewer prompted
Cesar Pelli to build a near-twin next door.
See p014

1600 Smith Street
Oddities in the street grid shape this tower
by architects Morris-Aubry, its staggered
setbacks culminating in an octagonal cap.
1600 Smith Street

INTRODUCTION
THE CHANGING FACE OF THE URBAN SCENE

Houston isn't an easy city to read. It sprawls over the Texas coastal plain, its freeways and suburbs spreading out for miles in every direction. From a speeding car (the way most people enter town), the view is mainly malls and billboards interrupted sporadically by office towers. It's the kind of landscape that prompts critics to dismiss Houston as a place with little sense of place. Sidestep the first impressions, though, and you'll see how wrong they are. This is a city on the rise. The restaurants are some of the most inventive in the country, the art scene is vibrant, and locals have access to more parkland than in any other American metropolis. Houston is bold and brash, and very Texan, but it values first-class museums and the performing arts as much as Big Oil and beer joints. The city thrives on contrasts, which is what makes a visit so interesting.

Without a doubt, two of the best things about Houston are its neighbourhoods and its people. The area that lies inside Interstate 610 (the Loop) is intensely community-oriented, with some districts feeling more like small towns than parts of the fourth largest city in the US. Its inhabitants are young (the median age is 32), diverse (more than 100 languages are spoken) and unfailingly friendly, and they give Houston a refreshingly laidback vibe.

Filtering through the layers of this destination is not always an easy task, but with a bit of effort and insider knowledge it can be great fun. This guide gives you a push in the right direction.

ESSENTIAL INFO

FACTS, FIGURES AND USEFUL ADDRESSES

TOURIST OFFICE
Houston Visitors Center
1st floor, 901 Bagby Street
T 713 437 5556
www.visithoustontexas.com

TRANSPORT
Airport transfer
SuperShuttle operates a door-to-door
service bookable in advance online
www.supershuttle.com
Bicycle rental
Bici
2309 Dunlavy Street
www.bici713.com
Car hire
Avis
George Bush Intercontinental Airport
T 281 443 5800
Metro
www.ridemetro.org
Taxis
Yellow Cab
T 713 236 1111
Travel card
A Metro day pass costs $3

EMERGENCY SERVICES
Emergencies
T 911
Police (non-emergencies)
T 713 884 3131
Late-night pharmacy
Walgreens
1919 W Gray Street
T 713 526 3621

CONSULATES
British Consulate-General
Suite 1900, 1000 Louisiana Street
T 713 659 6270
www.gov.uk/government/world/usa

POSTAL SERVICES
Post office
401 Franklin Street
T 713 226 3161
Shipping
UPS
945 McKinney Street
T 832 204 3767

BOOKS
Ephemeral City: Cite Looks at Houston
edited by Barrie Scardino, William F Stern
and Bruce C Webb (University of Texas)
Houston Architectural Guide by
Stephen Fox (AIA Houston)
Houston: It's Worth It (ttweak)

WEBSITES
Architecture
www.houstondeco.org
www.offcite.org
Newspapers
www.chron.com

EVENTS
Houston Art Car Parade
www.thehoustonartcarparade.com
Rice Design Alliance Architecture Tour
www.ricedesignalliance.org

COST OF LIVING
**Taxi from George Bush Intercontinental
Airport to city centre**
$53
Cappuccino
$3.50
Packet of cigarettes
$7
Daily newspaper
$1
Bottle of champagne
$60

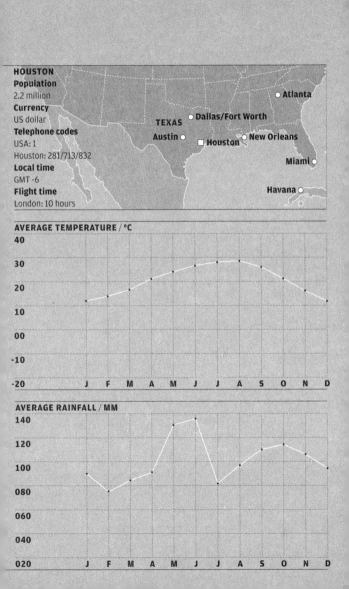

HOUSTON
Population
2.2 million
Currency
US dollar
Telephone codes
USA: 1
Houston: 281/713/832
Local time
GMT -6
Flight time
London: 10 hours

Atlanta

TEXAS · Dallas/Fort Worth

Austin · □ Houston · New Orleans

Miami

Havana

AVERAGE TEMPERATURE / °C

40
30
20
10
00
-10
-20

J F M A M J J A S O N D

AVERAGE RAINFALL / MM

140
120
100
080
060
040
020

J F M A M J J A S O N D

NEIGHBOURHOODS

THE AREAS YOU NEED TO KNOW AND WHY

To help you navigate the city, we've chosen the most interesting districts (see below and the map inside the back cover) and colour-coded our featured venues, according to their location; those venues that are outside these areas are not coloured.

HEIGHTS

Developed in the 1890s as an independent city, the Heights' Victorian cottages and bungalows give it a small-town feel (a 1912 anti-liquor law banishing bars to its edges helps keep things quiet). Head to W 19th Street, the area's 'downtown', lined with shops and eateries like Shade (see p042).

MIDTOWN

Young professionals pack into Midtown's trendy clubs and apartment blocks in the north end, which must deal with its vacant lots before it attains big-city glitz. The south end is grittier and more interesting, and includes landmark buildings such as Trinity Church (1015 Holman Street).

RIVER OAKS

Rich Houstonlans flocked to River Oaks in the 1920s, lured by the idea of creating an exclusive suburban community within view of Downtown. Their mansions, set amid manicured gardens, offer a crash course in Western domestic architecture. Visit Bayou Bend (1 Westcott Street, T 713 639 7750), a 1928 mansion-cum-museum.

DOWNTOWN

Business is the byword in the city's historic heart, although a decade of regeneration has added lofts, shops, hotels and stadia. The leisure options are mainly grouped around Market Square and the Theater District. The real highlight is the skyline, as seen from Buffalo Bayou (see p092).

RICE/MUSEUM DISTRICT

Main Street cuts through this pretty area, where pristine residential streets surround the quintessentially collegiate Rice campus. To the west is the compact Rice Village, a shoppers' haunt, and to the east Hermann Park, which acts as a buffer between the Museum District and Texas Medical Center.

WASHINGTON CORRIDOR

Once-hip bars and clubs situated along Washington Avenue, the district's main drag, are now the haunt of party-minded twentysomethings. However, some solid restaurant options remain, including Benjy's (5922 Washington Avenue, T 713 868 1131), good for drinks and a bite.

MONTROSE

Gentrification has dulled the edges of this 1960s and 1970s boho enclave, although Montrose still has its share of characterful boutiques, bars and cafés, such as Brasil (see p037). Eminently walkable, the area's modest scale and lack of pretension is exemplified by the Menil Collection museum (see p064), located on the south side.

UPTOWN

Houston's Uptown skyline, defined by the Williams Tower (see p010), is one of the largest clusters of high-rises in the country. At its heart is the 1969 Galleria shopping mall (see p072), a monument to consumerism patterned (loosely) after Milan's Galleria Vittorio Emanuele II.

LANDMARKS

THE SHAPE OF THE CITY SKYLINE

Houston's metropolitan straggle covers a relentlessly flat part of Texas, virtually unchecked by topography or any restrictions on land use. The attitude appears to be anything goes when it comes to the built environment here, which creates numerous contrasts in style and scale that are sometimes jarring, often magnificent and almost always architecturally fascinating.

The urban schizophrenia is due in part to the city's dizzying growth in the second half of the 20th century. Pre-1950, Houston was relatively compact, producing human-scale buildings such as the 1939 City Hall (see p011). Then everything changed. Fuelled by the oil industry and postwar optimism, the city exploded, and so did its builders' ambitions. Houston's postmodern skyscrapers, such as the Williams Tower (overleaf) and 1400 Smith Street (see p014), owe their shape to the same blend of ingenuity and civic pride that created the Astrodome, a vision of a futuristic, climate-controlled utopia now sadly threatened with demolition.

Today, planners are filling in the gaps left by this development and, in the process, creating Houston's own brand of urbanism. Of course, no amount of glass and steel beats nature. This subtropical city is actually very green, a blanket of trees covering a multitude of urban sins. The impression from above, of an enormous garden punctuated by ranks of distant high-rises, is surprisingly beautiful. *For full addresses, see Resources.*

Williams Tower

American developer Gerald Hines called his retail/hotel/business complex, The Galleria, 'a new downtown' when the first phase opened in 1969, and he spent the next decade or so surrounding it with office buildings to reinforce the idea. The culmination of that effort was the Williams Tower, a Johnson/Burgee-designed high-rise influenced by the art deco towers of the 1920s and 1930s. The architects faced the 275m structure in silver and black glass, topping it with a rotating beacon. The design is less successful at street level, where a huge (and incongruous) pink-granite entrance arch leads to a vast lobby. But no matter. The Williams Tower is best appreciated at a distance, its broad-shouldered silhouette leaving a silvery trace of Gotham in the sky.
2800 Post Oak Boulevard

City Hall

'We are building for the masses, not the classes,' Austrian-born architect Joseph Finger informed civic officials when he presented his plan for a new city hall. More than 70 years on, Finger's art deco edifice, completed in 1939, remains the city's functional and ceremonial centre, although the local government outgrew it long ago. Behind an angular limestone facade are Finger's best interiors, which include the blond walnut-panelled Council Room and a lobby lined with nickel, silver, bronze and coloured marble. True to its time, the building has its fair share of integrated artwork. There are allegorical murals on the lobby ceiling, by American artist and designer Daniel MacMorris, and, above the principal entrances, history's lawgivers are rendered in aluminium.

901 Bagby Street, T 713 437 5200

BG Group Place

This 46-storey skyscraper could have overwhelmed its historic neighbours; it's diagonally opposite the Gulf Building (see p057) and the princely 1915 Texas Company Building (720 San Jacinto Street). But its architects, Pickard Chilton, designed BG Group Place to be surprisingly deferential. The structure, finished in 2011, is wrapped in silver glass that reflects the surrounding cityscape. Its north and south facades are slightly curved, giving the 192m tower a graceful silhouette. The real plus, though, is its energy efficiency. Aluminium and glass fins help to shade offices from the sun, and water that condenses in the HVAC system is used to irrigate the sky gardens. The upper garden is at the base of the five-storey 'notch' on the east side, which is now a prominent feature of the skyline. *811 Main Street, www.bggroupplace.com*

Esperson Buildings

When the 125m Niels Esperson Building was completed in 1927, it was the tallest high-rise in Texas. Commissioned by Mellie Esperson, it also proved to be one of the most extravagant, boasting a polychrome terracotta exterior, and interiors in brass and marble (a lavish tribute to Mellie's late husband, Niels). New York architect John Eberson, best known for his movie palaces, gave the structure a theatrical design; its crown, a circular tempietto, is said to have been based on the Tomb of Mausolus. Eberson and his son, Drew, returned in 1941 to design a companion building (above left), more restrained than the first. Today, both house private offices, but the twin lobbies (one Renaissance flash, the other moderne sophistication) are publicly accessible in business hours. *808 Travis Street*

1400 Smith Street

Set among a clutch of corporate towers, the formerly named Four Allen Center became a symbol of corporate hubris when its then tenant, the energy company Enron, collapsed in 2001. Fortunately, enough time has elapsed for the 1983 building to emerge from Enron's shadow and be judged on its own merits. Houston-based architects Lloyd Jones Brewer designed a 50-storey modernist slab updated with elegant rounded ends, then encased the whole structure in silver glass and white aluminium, rotating it off the Downtown grid. The result is a highly reflective tower that is at once aggressive and elusive. The design worked so well that Cesar Pelli quoted it in a second tower (above left), completed in 2002. The two are connected by a low-level circular walkway.

1400 Smith Street

Chase Tower

The tallest structure in the state is the architectural equivalent of a finely tailored business suit: refined, precise and, if a 305m-high skyscraper can qualify, understated. IM Pei gave the building a compact footprint and sliced its south-west corner at a 45-degree angle, leaving two-thirds of the site for a public plaza that features *Personage and Birds*, the largest Joan Miró sculpture ever commissioned. The tower's granite walls soar from the ground, giving it a monolithic quality, but the details – the granite panels, windows aligned in perfect rows, a flash of stainless-steel trim – are worth viewing up close. The Sky Lobby on the 60th floor offers superb views; below ground, the building connects with Downtown's 11km of pedestrian tunnels. *600 Travis Street, www.chasetower.com*

HOTELS

WHERE TO STAY AND WHICH ROOMS TO BOOK

For years, the city's top hotels were stuffy affairs where overblown Europeana was the hallmark of luxury. Over the past decade or so, a smattering of design-led accommodation has arrived on the scene, offering an alternative to the sea of Hiltons and Hyatts.

The majority of the most stylish properties are located inside the Loop, making them convenient for exploring Houston's more interesting neighbourhoods. Downtown, Hotel Icon (see p020) resides within a restored bank building steps from Market Square, while the slick Sam Houston Hotel (1117 Prairie Street, T 832 200 8800), housed in a former stopover for travelling salesmen, dates to the 1920s. Further out, but still relatively central, are the ritzy Hotel ZaZa (see p021) in the Museum District, and the Modern B&B (see p022), a hip, under-the-radar option in Montrose. To the west, many hotels cater mainly to business guests. However, there are good rooms at Hotel Derek (2525 W Loop South, T 713 961 3000), a stone's throw from The Galleria (see p072), and Hotel Sorella (opposite), a surprisingly sleek choice in the suburbs.

Time will tell whether Houston attracts chicer hotels. There were rumours of new outposts of the luxury chains Ritz-Carlton, W and Le Méridien before the economic downturn, as well as talk of some intriguing boutique projects. Given the resurgence of the American energy market, they may finally see the light of day. *For full addresses and room rates, see Resources.*

Hotel Sorella

Due to its interiors by Peter Remedios and its position in the mixed-use CityCentre complex, the Sorella injected a shot of style into west Houston when it opened here in 2009. The modern decor in the lobby (overleaf) carries over into the 244 rooms, where darkwood furnishings and jewel tones play off white walls. Despite their floor-to-ceiling windows, some of the rooms can be dark; we suggest a Junior Suite or the Penthouse (above) for extra light and space. Useful amenities include passes to the adjacent Life Time Athletic (T 713 464 1200), a comprehensive gym and spa. Post-workout, have a drink at the hotel's ground-floor Bistro Bar (T 713 827 3545) – a quieter alternative to the Monnalisa lounge upstairs.
800 Sorella Court, T 713 973 1600,
www.hotelsorella-citycentre.com

Lobby, Hotel Sorella

Hotel Icon

If you're the type who likes a dash of early 20th-century opulence, check into the Icon, which is housed in a neoclassical 1912 bank building. San Francisco firm Candra Scott & Anderson made the most of a $35m restoration budget by outfitting the guest rooms with richly textured and patterned fabrics and wallpapers, wood panelling and marble, but kept things light with a modern palette and Texan touches,

such as steer's-head bathroom hooks. Guests who can afford to should splash out on an elegant 12th-floor suite, such as No 1215 (above), or the Penthouse, which has its own rooftop party area and terrace. Those without such deep pockets can console themselves at Line & Lariat, Icon's highly regarded in-house restaurant. *220 Main Street, T 713 224 4266, www.hotelicon.com*

Hotel ZaZa

Believers in 'less is more' should brace
themselves for the ZaZa, which brought
some offbeat charms to the Museum
District in 2007. Dallas-based firm Duncan
Miller Ullmann, in collaboration with
Z-Resorts' president, Benji Homsey, and
the hotel's founder, Charlie Givens, took
care of the interior design, which, as seen
in the lobby (above), mixes Baccarat
chandeliers and hand-carved panelling
with luxurious textiles. Beyond the excess,
the ZaZa is a fine hotel, with comfy, well-
appointed rooms. For its sheer decadence,
book a Magnificent Seven Suite like the
200 sq m Rock Star, which has mirrored
walls and two king-size beds. Downstairs,
the ZaSpa (T 713 639 4566) adjoins a pool
(see p094) that overlooks Hermann Park.
5701 Main Street, T 713 526 1991,
www.hotelzaza.com

Modern B&B

Houston needs more hotels like the
Modern, which is smartly designed
and tucked in a cool area. Of the eight
rooms, which occupy two townhouses
converted by Collins Architects, we like
the Treehouse. Expect hostess Lisa
Thompson to lead spirited discussions
over drinks in the lobby (pictured).
*4003 Hazard Street, T 832 279 6367,
www.modernbb.com*

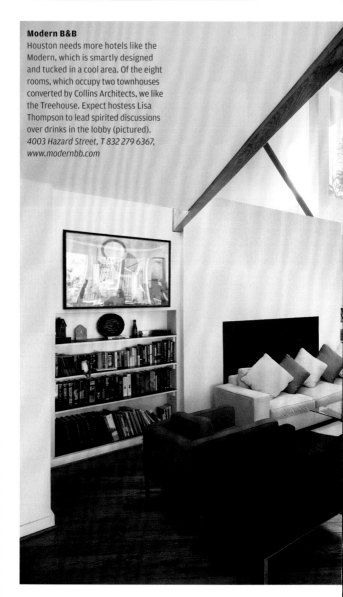

24 HOURS

SEE THE BEST OF THE CITY IN JUST ONE DAY

Art may not be the first thing that comes to mind when you think of Houston, but the city thrives on it. The scene is buzzing, diverse and sometimes strange. The more eccentric venues include the Orange Show Center for Visionary Art (2402 Munger Street, T 713 926 6368), the monument to a postal worker's lifelong obsession with oranges; the Art Car Museum (140 Heights Boulevard, T 713 861 5526); and Beer Can House (222 Malone Street, T 713 926 6368), a bungalow covered with more than 50,000 crushed beer cans (yes, one man did most of the drinking). Our itinerary takes in a pair of the city's major art venues (see p028 and p029), both in the Museum District. These are just two of 18 institutions there. Isamu Noguchi's Cullen Sculpture Garden (1001 Bissonnet Street, T 713 639 7300) is also recommended, and the nearby Lawndale Art Center (4912 Main Street, T 713 528 5858) and Houston Center for Photography (1441 W Alabama Street, T 713 529 4755) generally put on interesting exhibitions by local and mid-career artists.

We end the day with dinner at Oxheart (see p030), which has quickly risen to the top of Houston's burgeoning restaurant realm. If you are in the mood for partying, know that Houston does not do the velvet-rope scene well; far more rewarding are the bars around Market Square, including the historic La Carafe (see p031), and *mezcaleria* The Pastry War (310 Main Street, T 713 226 7770). *For full addresses, see Resources.*

09.30 Tiny Boxwood's

A café inside a nursery could take a turn towards twee, so it's fortunate that Tiny Boxwood's, in business since 2007, is so well done. The dining area and the patio give on to a small lawn via antique French windows; the see-and-be-seen seats are around the communal hammered-metal table in the centre of the room. Chef Baron Doke's menu favours lighter dishes over belt-busting Southern fare. We suggest an order of the migas (eggs scrambled with house-ground sausage, peppers, onions, potatoes and tortilla strips, and covered in salsa), and any or all of the homemade breads, muffins and jams. For a zesty start to the morning, also try an Orange Julia, a blend of orange-blossom honey, crushed ice and fresh orange juice. *3614 W Alabama Street, T 713 622 4224, www.tinyboxwoods.com*

11.00 Rothko Chapel

Philanthropists John and Dominique de Menil facilitated two of the best marriages of art and architecture in the city: the Menil Collection (see p064) and the Rothko Chapel, an ecumenical space designed to house 14 commissioned paintings by the artist Mark Rothko. Howard Barnstone and Eugene Aubry's 1971 building is a minimal structure with greyish-pink brick walls and black-steel accents. The canvases inside seem equally plain at first glance, but soon reveal numerous colours and shapes when viewed in the diffused natural light. Outside, Barnett Newman's 1967 sculpture *Broken Obelisk* (opposite), which the Menils dedicated as a memorial to the civil rights leader Dr Martin Luther King Jr, rises out of a reflecting pool. Open daily, 10am to 6pm. *3900 Yupon Street, T 713 524 9839, www.rothkochapel.org*

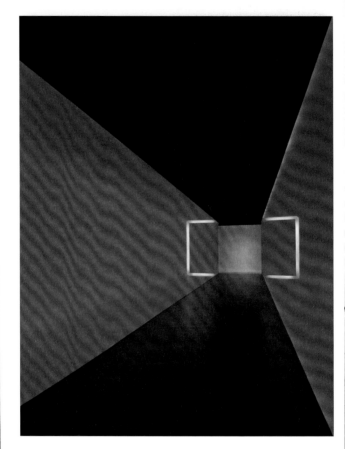

12.30 The Light Inside

California-based artist James Turrell's 1999 installation *The Light Inside* makes an underground pedestrian tunnel at the Museum of Fine Arts (see p060) anything but pedestrian. Concealed neon tubing turns the 36m-long walls from scarlet to blue and back again, while an elevated walkway creates a sense of vertigo. The effect is both calming and disorientating. Within the museum complex, architect Rafael Moneo's classically influenced Beck Building galleries and Mies van der Rohe's 1958 Cullinan Hall are excellent places to view art, especially exhibitions based on MFAH's growing Latin American collection. A good spot for lunch is Cafe Express (T 713 639 7370) on the Beck Building's lower level. Closed Mondays. *1001 Bissonnet Street, T 713 639 7300, www.mfah.org*

15.00 Contemporary Arts Museum

Houston has a long tradition of offbeat art, which influences the shows at the Contemporary Arts Museum (it has no permanent collection of its own). The exhibits are sometimes impressive and sometimes forgettable, but they rarely fail to push the artistic envelope one way or another – worth the gamble when entry is free. Michigan architects Gunnar Birkerts enclosed the double-volume main gallery in a parallelogram of corrugated stainless steel, allowing the museum to assert its presence on a prominent corner, even as it defers to Mies' Brown Pavilion (see p060) across the street. The basement galleries can be claustrophobic, but they have the saving grace of being adjacent to the excellent CAMH shop. Closed Mondays. *5216 Montrose Boulevard, T 713 284 8250, www.camh.org*

20.00 Oxheart

Since its 2012 launch, Oxheart has earned international praise, and deservedly so. Chef Justin Yu draws diners eager to try a trio of tasting menus (one meat or fish, one vegetarian and a third with a bit of everything) featuring local produce cooked in a modern American style. The dishes change constantly but often incorporate ingredients such as goose, catfish, okra and sweet potatoes, which are prepared and paired to bring out surprisingly rich flavours. Accompanied by a global wine list and desserts by Yu's wife, pastry chef Karen Man, this is some of the finest food in the US. The interior, by Gin Braverman, sets salvaged-pine and -cedar furnishings against exposed brick and concrete. Closed Tuesdays and Wednesdays.

1302 Nance Street, T 832 830 8592, www.oxhearthouston.com

23.00 La Carafe

It may not be the oldest bar in Houston but, thanks to its home in a narrow brick building dating to 1861, La Carafe feels as if it has been around forever. (It's actually been here since 1962.) The wonderfully dim interior is all dark wood, crumbling plaster and creaky floors, and has the kind of patina that comes only with longevity and a steady stream of regulars. Neither the wine nor beer list is the most striking in town, but watching the sun sink over Market Square and the Downtown towers from the balcony certainly compensates. After dark, pull up a stool at the downstairs bar and join the clientele of local workers, theatregoers and couriers. You could end up in a discussion about the memorabilia on the walls – providing the bartender produces a flashlight so you can see it.
813 Congress Street, T 713 229 9399

URBAN LIFE

CAFÉS, RESTAURANTS, BARS AND NIGHTCLUBS

Houston's dining scene is attracting worldwide attention for good reason. Thanks to a group of young chefs and the diverse palate of a multicultural population, eating out in the city has never been more exciting. For proof, head to Oxheart (see p030), Underbelly (see p040), Chris Shepherd's homage to local cooking, and The Pass and Provisions (opposite), which casts a broader net with its new American menu. And, of course, there is the Texas holy trinity of steak, barbecue and Tex-Mex: try Gatlin's (1221 W 19th Street, T 713 869 4227); tuck into a plate of enchiladas at El Real (1201 Westheimer Road, T 713 524 1201); or stop by Chuy's (see p043) for a healthy dollop of kitsch. Houston's myriad ethnic restaurants, many tucked away in strip malls, are also worth exploring. Vieng Thai (6929 Long Point Road, T 713 688 9910) is one of the best.

The nightlife is just as vibrant, but choose your venue carefully. Head Downtown or to Montrose for the greatest concentrations of atmospheric bars and pubs. The West Alabama Ice House (1919 W Alabama Street, T 713 528 6874) has been around for years, while more recent venues include the wine bar Camerata (see p034) and cocktail hotspots Anvil (1424 Westheimer Road, T 713 523 1622) and Goro & Gun (306 Main Street, T 832 708 6195). Many cafés also pull double shifts as bars; check out Lowbrow (1601 W Main Street, T 281 501 8288) and Down House (1801 Yale Street, T 713 864 3696). *For full addresses, see Resources.*

The Pass and Provisions

Chefs Seth Siegel-Gardner and Terrence Gallivan, both veterans of kitchens in New York, Chicago and London, opened something unique in Houston in 2012: two restaurants, the casual Provisions and upscale The Pass (above), each served by a common kitchen but offering very different dining experiences. The concept works extremely well. At Provisions, the wood-burning oven turns out an array of roasted meat, fish and pizzas for lunch or dinner, and there is a broad wine, beer and cocktail list. The Pass is built around two sophisticated tasting menus based on inventive dishes such as venison infused with coffee and served with swede. The crisp, pitch-perfect interiors are the work of Betty Maccagnan of MB Simple.
807 Taft Street, T 713 628 9020, www.passandprovisions.com

Camerata

Restaurateur Paul Petronella ticked all the boxes for an inner-Loop wine bar when he opened Camerata in 2013. It has a prime location between Montrose and River Oaks, a modish interior, a relaxed atmosphere, and a wide-ranging wine list assembled by sommelier David Keck. The happy-hour deal is one of the best in town, offering half-price glasses from bottles opened the previous night. Houston designer Gin Braverman gave the space an industrial edge, installing a concrete bar, although touches like the communal table and tiled alphabet on the back-bar wall, used to sort open tabs, avoid any pretension. Visit Petronella's popular café, Paulie's, next door, and order some homemade pasta or its signature shrimp BLT sandwich. *1834 Westheimer Road, T 713 807 7271, www.pauliesrestaurant.com/camerata*

Reef

Bryan Caswell and Bill Floyd are not new to the local restaurant scene, but truly hit their stride with this seafood house. Houston firm Office for Design based the interiors of the former car dealership on an oyster, treating the exposed beams and concrete-and-terrazzo floor as the shell, and adding pearlescent tables and capiz-shell chandeliers as the treasure inside. The steel-and-glass wine cellar showcases Floyd's superb list, which includes a page of bottles that have Houston links, and the market-style fish room affords a glimpse of the kitchen. Here, Caswell (a fisherman himself) does clever things, often using varieties, like wahoo and croaker, rarely seen on city menus. Reef stands out in a genre where innovation is in short supply. *2600 Travis Street, T 713 526 8282, www.reefhouston.com*

Brasil

When Dan Fergus bought this former bike shop in 1992, he'd planned on creating a Brazilian folk-art gallery, but it ended up morphing into a café/bar. Lucky for us, as it remains one of the best hangouts in Montrose. The relaxed atmosphere and the solid drinks list contribute to Brasil's success, as does the no-fuss menu. For breakfast, order the prosciutto, bacon, or salmon eggs Benedict; for lunch or dinner, try a goat's cheese and beetroot sandwich, or any of the pizzas (the one with rocket, mozzarella and marinated figs is popular). The streetside patio is good for people watching, but we prefer the leafy area at the back, where Brasil and neighbouring art space The Brandon (see p054) screen films when the weather is fine.
2604 Dunlavy Street, T 713 528 1993, www.cafe-brasil.net

Local Foods

There is a lot to like about this airy deli with a locavore credo, owned by the team behind Benjy's (T 713 522 7602) next door. Order one of the excellent sandwiches, such as the blue crab and shrimp, and a 24-hour cold-brew coffee. A bite to eat here, coupled with a visit to Benjy's upstairs lounge, is an ideal introduction to the Rice Village.
2424 Dunstan Road, T 713 521 7800

Underbelly

'The story of Houston food' is Underbelly's declaration of intent. Chef Chris Shepherd has duly created a menu that celebrates the city's culinary diversity, with touches of Asia, the Med and the American South, and his ingredients are sourced from local farmers, ranchers and fishermen. The result is a restaurant that is uniquely Houstonian, from its farmhouse-themed interior (the work of Collaborative Projects) to the daily changing menu, which features dishes such as Korean braised goat and dumplings. Matthew Pridgen's extensive wine list exclusively includes bottles from family-owned or -operated wineries, and describes them with considerable wit. Finish your meal off with a piece of vinegar pie, a surprisingly tasty American classic. *1100 Westheimer Road, T 713 528 9800, www.underbellyhouston.com*

D&T Drive Inn

Before home refrigerators were common, Texans acquired their ice from icehouses, neighbourhood establishments that often doubled as beer joints. They're a vanishing breed but, happily, D&T is an exception. Restaurateurs Joey Treadway and Chris Cusack bought this venue in 2012 and spent the next year returning it to its late 1950s splendour, complete with cedar cladding and the original insulated ice-room door.

The interior got a mod-rustic makeover, with a bar handcrafted from a tree out back and retro-style seating by designer Haden Garrett. There are 50 Texan beers on tap, plus a frozen sangria and shandy. The short menu rounds things out with throwback dishes like Frito pie (beef stew, corn chips, jalapeños and pimento cheese). *1307 Enid Street, T 713 868 6165, www.treadsack.com/dtdriveinn*

Shade

Claire Smith and Russell Murrell's Shade brought an easy sophistication to Heights when it opened here in 2003. A decade or so on, it has competition but remains a bright spot on the neighbourhood dining scene, serving shoppers on 19th Street by day and becoming a dinner destination at night. Designer Ferenc Dreef's painted ceiling trusses and soft green accents provide a low-key yet refined setting for the new American menu by Gregg Beebe. The food isn't revolutionary, but it doesn't need to be when it's prepared this well. There's a solid wine list that leans heavily on California, although you'll have to join Shade's 'private club' to sample it – a free and painless way around Heights' old but still active anti-alcohol bylaw.
250 W 19th Street, T 713 863 7500,
www.shadeheights.com

Chuy's

Houstonians never tire of debating where to find the finest Tex-Mex in town, but most would agree that the River Oaks branch of Chuy's takes the crown for best decor. It's a riot of over-the-topness, with 1950s-style seating, lava lamps and velvet paintings in the main dining room. The menu comprises a fairly straightforward selection; lavish portions reach their zenith in the Elvis Presley Memorial Combo, which includes three types of enchiladas, a taco, chilli con carne, and rice and beans. The wait for a table can be long (happy hour starts early), but it's hard to be too impatient while sipping an oversized margarita and munching on complimentary nachos, all served from the boot of a glorious vintage car parked up against the wall. *2706 Westheimer Road, T 713 524 1700, www.chuys.com*

Canopy

Claire Smith and Russell Murrell, who also
own Shade (see p042), took inspiration
from Houston's live oak trees for their
second restaurant. The name references
the leafy coverage of the surrounding
Montrose area, and the double-volume
dining room, with an earth-toned floor,
sky-blue walls, wood accents and pops of
green, reinforces the idea. Locally based
architect Dillon Kyle designed the space,
including the bird's nest of wooden rails
suspended from the ceiling. The kitchen
turns out consistently good breakfast,
lunch and dinner dishes that combine
flavours from Texas and the greater Gulf
Coast, reflecting Houston's wide-ranging
culinary scene. At the weekend, brunch
is served from 9am until 3pm.
*3939 Montrose Boulevard, T 713 528 6848,
www.canopyhouston.com*

Triniti

What surprises about Triniti, considering its carefully composed interior, food and service, is how accessible it is. Elsewhere, a similar combination may call for dressing up and advance bookings, but not here. Credit for the design goes to MC2, who wrapped the former dry cleaner's building in a perforated metal skin and installed two-tone walnut furniture and Tom Dixon lighting inside; the art on display includes works by Tseng Kwong Chi (opposite) and Todd Murphy (above). The modern American menu follows Triniti's concept of 'savoury, sweet and spirits'. Veal *osso buco* is served with an almond *horchata*, a Mexican-inspired sauce; and the zesty Broken Clock cocktail is made with gin, grapefruit, raspberry and jalapeño.
2815 S Shepherd Drive, T 713 527 9090, www.trinitirestaurant.com

Cuchara

There's no shortage of Tex-Mex in town, but few restaurants are twisting classic Mexican cuisine like Cuchara. Based on recipes handed down from co-owner Ana Beaven's Mexican grandmother, the menu has meat, fish and veggie options; the *comida corrida* lunch (three courses served with an *agua fresca*) is a good way to sample it. Where Cuchara truly shines is in its small plates and cocktails. Order some south-of-the-border staples such as *charalitos* (slightly salty fried lake fish served with salsa), paired with a Bandido, a concoction of sotol (a smoky spirit from Chihuahua), lemon juice, Pimm's and chia seeds. The dining room, which features murals by Beaven's sister, Cecilia, was designed by Collaborative Projects.
214 Fairview Street, T 713 942 0000, www.cuchararestaurant.com

Southside Espresso

Interesting coffee culture can be hard to find in a city where there seems to be a Starbucks on every corner. For good joe, head to Montrose and this café tucked behind Japanese restaurant Uchi (T 713 522 4808). Opened in 2012 in a former landmark Tex-Mex restaurant (the painted ceiling beams are a hangover from those days), Southside serves Fusion Beans coffee, roasted by owner Sean Marshall, along with rotating selections from other top American roasters. There's also a short but well-chosen list of wines and local beers, and baked goods from Houston's Clean Sweets. The venue is small, but you can usually get a seat at the bar or on one of Southside's attractive patios – there's one streetside and another on the roof.
904c Westheimer Road, T 713 942 9990,
www.southsideespresso.com

Sparrow Bar + Cookshop
Chef Monica Pope caught everyone's
eye when she opened T'afia in Midtown
in 2002. Now, Pope has turned it into
Sparrow. The local and seasonal menu
retains many popular dishes, and the
bar food and cocktails are especially
good. The interior, by Installations
Antiques and Sara Eliason features
custom-made and reclaimed elements.
3701 Travis Street, T 713 524 6922

13 Celsius

Local wine bars come and go, but 13 Celsius has stood its ground thanks to its tightly edited drinks list and stylish vibe. Co-owned by Mike Sammons and Ian Rosenberg, it's housed in a restored 1920s dry-cleaning shop. Rosenberg oversaw the design, stripping the interior down to its stucco walls and tin ceiling. Furniture reclaimed from the old Warwick Hotel, now the ZaZa (see p021), and a vintage deli counter helped to create a space that's both raw and urbane. Pull up a seat at the marble bar for a view of the cellar and maximum interaction with the staff, who will guide you through the wines, beers, cheeses and charcuterie. The duo's other venture, beer and cocktail bar Mongoose versus Cobra (T 713 650 6872), is nearby. *3000 Caroline Street, T 713 529 8466, www.13celsius.com*

The Continental Club

For live music in an intimate setting with a distinctly Texan feel, there's no better place in Houston than this version of the famous Austin club. The building housed a general store in the 1920s, and the venue, which opened in 2000, has retained the original light fixtures and pressed-tin ceiling. The touring and Houston-based acts on the bill tend towards country, rock and combinations of the two, and the themed nights draw a loyal following. Barbecue is served amid the pool tables in the back room (above), and there's a big patio if you want to escape the noise. The club shares this stretch of Main Street with a variety of retail outlets that are worth checking out, including the quirky record shop Sig's Lagoon (T 713 533 9525). *3700 Main Street, T 713 529 9899, www.continentalclub.com*

INSIDER'S GUIDE
AIMEE HEIMBINDER, DESIGN CONSULTANT

Raised in rural Texas, Aimee Heimbinder worked in fashion and advertising in New York before settling in Houston. She's a fan of the local art scene, particularly galleries such as Art Palace (3913 Main Street, T 281 501 2964), which specialises in rising Texan talent, and contemporary-focused Montrose space The Brandon (1709 Westheimer Road, T 713 522 0369). Not surprisingly, her taste in shopping runs to design-forward stores like Laboratoria (2803 Westheimer Road, T 832 407 2832), which she appreciates for its hard-to-source clothing lines. She also admires midcentury interiors shop Cool Stuff (1718 Westheimer Road, T 713 523 5222) and Kuhl-Linscomb (2424 W Alabama Street, T 713 526 6000), a huge emporium known for its range of books and homewares.

When it comes to food, Heimbinder savours the namesake salad at Indian café Pondicheri (Suite B132, 2800 Kirby Drive, T 713 522 2022) and visits Revival Market (550 Heights Boulevard, T 713 880 8463) to buy its house-cured charcuterie. If she's craving Texan fare, she calls into Goode Company Barbeque (5109 Kirby Drive, T 713 522 2530) or Ninfa's (2704 Navigation Boulevard, T 713 228 1175), famous for its *tacos al carbon* – flour tortillas stuffed with grilled beef or chicken. A 'precision-made' cocktail at Anvil (see p032) or a drink at estimable Downtown dive Warren's Inn (307 Travis Street, T 713 247 9207) is always a good way to end the day. *For full addresses, see Resources.*

ARCHITOUR

A GUIDE TO HOUSTON'S ICONIC BUILDINGS

Early Houston was a modest frontier village; floods, fires and time have left only a few scattered reminders of this, such as the Pillot Building (1012 Congress Street). During the oil boom of the 1920s, planners began to reject a traditional Southern look in favour of a modern style, as represented by the Gulf Building (opposite) and the LD Allen residence (2337 Blue Bonnet Boulevard).

   The city's midcentury movement began in earnest in 1948, when art patrons Dominique and John de Menil asked architect Philip Johnson to design their home, the Menil House (3363 San Felipe Street). A number of superlative structures followed, such as Mies van der Rohe's Cullinan Hall, part of the Museum of Fine Arts (see p060), and SOM's 1963 Tennessee Building, now called the Kinder Morgan Building (1010 Milam Street). Local firms added their own brands of modernity; two of the finest examples are the Jefferson Chemical Company Building (see p068), designed by Neuhaus & Taylor, and Caudill Rowlett Scott's 1966 Jones Hall (615 Louisiana Street, T 832 487 7050). Later, Johnson/Burgee's Pennzoil Place (see p066) and Republic Bank Center, now the Bank of America Center (700 Louisiana Street), led the way to a postmodern skyline.

   Currently, the city has a tendency to demolish many of its older buildings. Hopefully, in future, Houstonians will start to appreciate their architectural legacy before more of it is reduced to memory. *For full addresses, see Resources.*

Gulf Building

In his commission for this city landmark (now called the JP Morgan Chase Building after its principal tenant), businessman Jesse Jones specified a 'strikingly modern style and commanding height'. Houston architect Alfred C Finn delivered, creating a quintessentially art deco 130m high-rise that enjoyed the title of tallest building in town for more than 30 years following its completion in 1929. The quasi-Gothic exterior is Finn's tribute to Eliel Saarinen's never-realised design for Chicago's Tribune Tower. Inside, the lobby and three-storey limestone banking hall, open to the public during business hours, are the best deco interiors in the city. Don't miss Vincent Maragliotti's lobby frescoes chronicling the history of Texas, including a fanciful version of jazz age Houston.
712 Main Street

Chapel of St Basil

When Philip Johnson's Chapel of St Basil was dedicated at the University of St Thomas in 1997, someone suggested it was a better building than he would have designed 40 years earlier, when he was working on the university's campus plan and original architectural scheme. 'I'm a better architect than I was then,' Johnson retorted – and the chapel bears that out. The structure is formally straightforward, its body a white stucco block topped by a gold dome. Drama comes from a black granite plane that slices through at a 30-degree angle, defining the interior space and uniting the building with the steel arcade that rings Johnson's Academic Mall. Inside the chapel, art by Texan David Cargill is highlighted by natural light.
University of St Thomas, T 713 525 3589, www.stthom.edu

Museum of Fine Arts

Mies van der Rohe's 1954 masterplan for MFAH transformed a classical 1920s building into a modernist masterpiece. The first phase, the 1958 Cullinan Hall, enclosed a courtyard to create a soaring gallery space; the second, the 1974 Brown Pavilion (above), with Alexander Calder's 1962 sculpture *The Crab* outside, wrapped the hall in a gently curving wing with a steel-and-glass facade. The detailing is impeccable, from the green terrazzo flooring referencing the area's stately oaks to the steel columns and limestone facing an interpretation of William Ward Watkin's original exterior. The museum opened a major extension, Rafael Moneo's Beck Building, in 2000; another annexe is due to be designed by Steven Holl. *1001 Bissonnet Street, T 713 639 7300, www.mfah.org*

Asia Society Texas Center

Yoshio Taniguchi's first freestanding building in the US is a study in precision. The proportions are just so, the sightlines perfectly composed, and the materials painstakingly selected. The cherrywood panelling in the Great Hall, for example, was all taken from a single tree to ensure a consistent pattern. And yet the Asia Society Texas Center, completed in 2011, doesn't come across as cold or aloof.

On the contrary, its features combine to create a space that is warm and engaging. There's a full slate of exhibitions, concerts and lectures dedicated to Eastern culture, but visitors are also free simply to observe the architecture (the café makes a great lunch stop). Stop to take in the view of the skyline from the Water Garden Terrace. *1370 Southmore Boulevard, T 713 496 9901, www.asiasociety.org/texas*

Menil Collection
Renzo Piano's 1987 Menil Collection
museum (his debut US building) is one
of Houston's most quietly remarkable
structures. Its long, low massing and
grey-and-white exterior respect the
surrounding bungalows, and an elegant
system of ferroconcrete roof baffles
washes the galleries with natural light.
*1533 Sul Ross Street, T 713 525 9400,
www.menil.org*

Pennzoil Place

Johnson/Burgee's brief for a new Pennzoil HQ was fairly simple: to create a building that did not look like rival oil company Shell's boxy, travertine-clad tower. The architects' response was a pair of bronze glass trapezoids cut through the centre at a 45-degree angle and separated by a 3m gap running from the ground to the apex. Seeing the gap from a distance is interesting enough, but experiencing it at arm's length in the lobby is especially striking. The 1975 Pennzoil Place changed the Houston skyline and taught other architects that skyscrapers need not be Miesian glass boxes. Its stunning geometry, beautiful up close, may be even more engaging when seen from a car, making it perhaps the ideal landmark in a city where so much time is spent on the road.
711 Louisiana Street

Link-Lee Mansion

When Houston developer John Wiley Link completed his mansion in 1912, it was so splendid that locals claimed it had solid-gold doorknobs. That wasn't true, but it showed Link had hit his mark: he meant the house to be not only his family home but also a billboard for Montrose, his new suburban neighbourhood. Architects Sanguinet, Staats & Barnes of Fort Worth made the building stand out by virtue of its size (it was the largest private home in the city then) and by covering it in gleaming white brick, colourful tiles and enamelled terracotta, a sharp contrast to the Georgian 'country house' style that was popular at the time. Today, it contains offices for the University of St Thomas, which maintains the elaborate interiors. It's open to the public on weekdays.
3800 Montrose Boulevard , T 713 522 7911

Jefferson Chemical Company Building
Completed in 1965, this is the most refined
of the strip of 1960s office blocks that it
anchors, a last gasp of smaller-scale grace
before the area erupted with a variety of
squarish skyscrapers. Architects Neuhaus
& Taylor began with a four-storey black-
glass rectangle, then surrounded it with
slender columns that flare into plaster
vaults. The columns are similar to those
that Minoru Yamasaki designed for the
Northwestern National Life Building in
Minneapolis, completed the year before
this one. Whereas Yamasaki arranged
his to form a deep entry porch, Neuhaus
& Taylor used theirs to create screens on
all four facades, helping the Jefferson
to address its site at a hectic intersection.
The continuous colonnade suggests a
Greek temple, a concept strengthened
by the building's elevated position atop
a partially underground car park.
3336 Richmond Avenue

Brochstein Pavilion, Rice University
Completed in 2008, Thomas Phifer and
Partners' café pavilion brought new
life to a once desolate area of the Rice
campus. Floor-to-ceiling glass and a
light-filtering roof create a continuous
visual sweep between the interior and
exterior spaces, drawing attention away
from the building and down the row of
oak trees that frame the western lawn.
6100 Main Street, T 713 348 2279

SHOPPING

THE BEST RETAIL THERAPY AND WHAT TO BUY

Houston has long been a mall town, which is why most visiting shoppers will be directed to Uptown's 223,000 sq m Galleria (5085 Westheimer Road, T 713 622 0663); it is a high-end example, but a mall nonetheless. However, there are far more interesting stores to be found in the areas around Montrose and Rice University.

Jewellery and accessories shop Saint Cloud (5217 Kelvin Drive, T 713 522 0077) and menswear store The Class Room (see p076) stand out in the strollable Rice Village, while keen cyclists will find much to like at Montrose bike boutique Bici (2309 Dunlavy Street, T 713 522 8330). No tour of this district should omit the Texas Junk Company (215 Welch Street, T 713 524 6257), which carries a huge stock of secondhand cowboy gear, and the midcentury furniture dealer Reeves Antiques (2415 Taft Street, T 713 523 5577).

Label-conscious River Oaks boasts women's store Laboratoria (see p054), Southern designer Billy Reid (2702 Westheimer Road, T 713 552 0333), outposts of Atlanta retailers Sid Mashburn (3272 Westheimer Road, T 713 936 9502) and Ann Mashburn (2515 River Oaks Boulevard, T 713 936 9503), and Sloan/Hall (see p080), seller of covetable objects and accessories. To the north, the Heights is heavy on antiques markets and cutesy boutiques; vintage clothing emporiums Retropolis (321 W 19th Street, T 713 861 1950) and Replay (373 W 19th Street, T 713 863 9344) are worth browsing. *For full addresses, see Resources.*

Hamilton Shirts

Houston's oldest family-owned business has been producing impeccable men's shirts since 1883. Most of Hamilton's output is directed to upmarket retailers, but its bespoke service is what has drawn generations of oilmen and cattle barons. Some 500 Italian and Swiss fabrics are held in stock at the clubby store (overleaf), and many more are available to order, including the full Thomas Mason Platinum line. Prices for bespoke orders reach up to $495 each; the shirts are all produced in the on-site workshop in about three weeks and can be shipped anywhere. A pair of boxer shorts made from fabric ends ($30) could offer the ultimate in coordination. This ready-to-wear Navy Bengal Stripe dress shirt (above) costs $245.

5700 Richmond Avenue, T 713 780 8222, www.hamiltonshirts.com

The Class Room

There's been something of a menswear boom in Houston in recent years, with shops such as Rye 51 (T 713 523 8222) on the edge of the River Oaks district and Reserve Supply Company (T 713 750 9582) in Washington Corridor doing their bit to improve locals' sartorial style. Launched in November 2011, The Class Room is noteworthy for its shop (the work of local designer Renee Galang) and its carefully selected stock. The clothes reflect the owners' passion for streetwear and classic American brands. There are several US lines here, including Gitman Vintage and Gant Rugger, alongside a solid selection of denim and limited-edition accessories. It's a formula that many men's shops have adopted but few carry off so well.
2534 Amherst Street, T 713 874 0004, www.theclassroomshop.com

Settlement

Husband-and-wife graphic designers Gene and Jenny Morgan, and interior designer Alicia Redman, opened Settlement in 2012 to showcase clothing, accessories and homewares designed and made in the US. This is a retail gap in Houston – numerous stores favour imports over indigenous products. Settlement's stock spans from men's shirts by the Washington DC-based designer Read Wall to womenswear by Kain Label and limited-edition jewellery by Dirty Librarian Chains of Brooklyn. The lofty interior, designed by Redman in collaboration with locally based firms Dumptruck Design and Forest Design Build, treads the line between raw and refined with aplomb. Time will tell whether other shops in Houston follow Settlement's retail model – we certainly hope so.
Suite M, 3939 Montrose Boulevard, T 713 701 7872, www.settlementgoods.com

Sloan/Hall

It's nigh on impossible to leave Marcus
Sloan and Shannon Hall's shop without
purchasing something. The well-curated
selection of jewellery and womenswear
is complemented by skincare products,
stationery, art and design books, as well
as more unusual offerings, making it
an ideal place to pick up a one-off gift.
*2620 Westheimer Road, T 713 942 0202,
www.sloanhall.com*

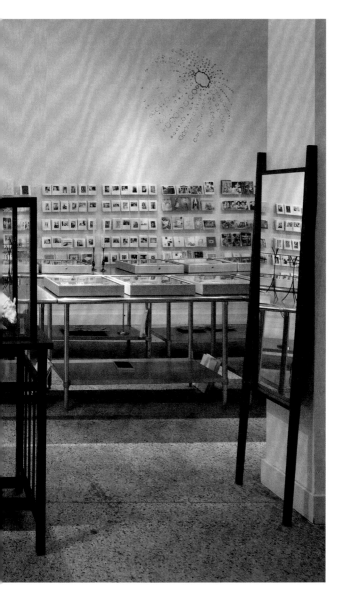

Crave Cupcakes
This shop may be one of the best-looking bakeries you'll see. New York-based firm AvroKO used white subway tiles to cover some of the walls and installed a glass display screen that allows views into the kitchen. The cupcakes are sublime, and are made from natural ingredients. Crave partner Elizabeth Harrison adapted recipes inherited from her grandmother. The baking is done in small batches, so nothing on the shelves is more than two hours old. All the products are available to go, but we recommend enjoying a Red Velvet at the counter, with some ice-cold milk from the shop's fountain. The fresh-fruit varieties are also heavenly. There's a second branch located near Rice Village.
1151-06 Uptown Park Boulevard,
T 713 622 7283, www.cravecupcakes.com

The Tipping Point

Its high ceilings, clean lines and recessed display scheme make this Downtown shop feel gallery-like, although here the art comes in the form of collectible treads, including Nikes, Pumas, PF Flyers and Rockwell by Parra. This is far more than a destination for trainer-heads, though. Opened in 2007 on the ground floor of a historic skyscraper, The Tipping Point was Houston's first lifestyle store, stocking books, art, accessories and music, and hosting frequent cultural events centred around the theory that small groups of early adopters have the ability to effect change. Founders David Rodriguez and Thomas Nauls took the store's name from the title of Malcolm Gladwell's book, which popularised this idea in 2000.
1212 Main Street, T 713 655 0443,
www.thetippingpointstore.com

Sicardi Gallery

Although Texan artists have long gained inspiration from south of the border, Latin American art remained underappreciated in Houston for years. This was partly why Buenos Aires native María Inés Sicardi opened her gallery here in 1994. Initially, her focus was on Argentinian painters, but she has since expanded to represent a variety of creatives from the region. Today, her space is one of the leading showcases for modern and contemporary Latin American art, exhibiting emerging as well as established figures such as Carlos Cruz-Diez (*Transchromie Dames A*, above) and Gego. The distinctive building (overleaf), designed by Houston's Brave Architecture, houses an art research centre in addition to two gallery spaces.
1506 W Alabama Street, T 713 529 1313, www.sicardi.com

SPORTS AND SPAS
WORK OUT, CHILL OUT OR JUST WATCH

Sport borders on a religion in Texas, so it's no surprise Houston has pumped generous sums into arenas for its professional teams, including the massive Reliant Stadium (1 Reliant Parkway, T 832 667 1400) used for American football. None are as iconic, though, as Wood and Zapata's Soldier Field in Chicago or Norman Foster's Wembley Stadium in London, but they are packed for nearly every game. Reliant does double duty as the host venue for the Houston Livestock Show and Rodeo (www.hlsr.com), which is held annually in March and is the largest of its kind in the world. Part competition, part carnival, it's not to be missed if you're in town.

Houston also has a fair range of options for personal recreation. The city's 23,000 hectares of parkland are a good start. Hermann Park (6001 Fannin Street) comprises gardens, a golf course and the Houston Zoo (T 713 533 6500), whereas Memorial Park (6501 Memorial Drive) offers hiking, cycling and jogging trails that tie into Buffalo Bayou Park (see p092). By 2015, half of this area will be landscaped, and half returned to wetlands and prairie, all of it affording fantastic views of the skyline. You can explore the park on foot or rent a bike from the B-cycle station (190 Sabine Street). For more refined R&R, book into the Trellis spa (opposite), or head to Hotel ZaZa (see p094) or the Four Seasons (1300 Lamar Street, T 713 650 1300) for a swim and some first-class people watching. *For full addresses, see Resources.*

Trellis, The Spa at The Houstonian

It is difficult to believe that Trellis at The Houstonian is just blocks from the clamour of Uptown – the spa, hotel and adjacent athletic club feel secluded on their wooded seven-hectare site near Memorial Park. Houston architects Kirksey designed the Mediterranean-style building to take full advantage of the setting, with large windows giving on to a courtyard. There's a generous array of treatments for both men and women using products by Carita and Decléor. For the works, book the Pure Bliss package: facial, manicure, shampoo and blow-dry, make-up, meal and 'tension relief cocoon' (a marine mud wrap), for $385. Minimalists may find fault with the button-down posh interior, but an hour or two here should quell any complaints. *111 North Post Oak Lane, T 713 685 6790, www.trellisspa.com*

Rice Stadium
Lloyd & Morgan and Milton McGinty's
70,000-seat stadium for Rice University,
which was constructed in an incredible
nine months to be operational in time
for the 1950 American football season,
is testament to the importance of the
sport in Texas. The upper decks are set
on slender concrete pillars, giving the
east and west facades a real elegance.
2176 University Boulevard, T 713 522 6957

Buffalo Bayou Park
This new greenbelt is the realisation of
a century-old plan to transform a section
of Buffalo Bayou into an urban resource.
A recent $58m push overseen by architects
SWA Group has resulted in 3.7km of public
promenades, art parks, hike/bike trails
and amenities such as Jamail Skatepark
(pictured), designed by the Seattle firm
Gridline. Completion is due by mid-2015.
Allen Parkway, www.buffalobayoupark.org

Hotel ZaZa pool
The stylish urban oasis at Hotel ZaZa
(see p021) – an elliptic pool, a terrace
and a bar overlooking Main Street – is
equal parts tropical resort and pure LA.
The lounge chairs arranged across the
broad terrace are prime spots at the
weekend, when waitresses circulate
with drinks and chilled scented towels.
*5701 Main Street, T 713 526 1991,
www.hotelzaza.com*

ESCAPES

WHERE TO GO IF YOU WANT TO LEAVE TOWN

Texas is 1,287km across at its widest point, so expect to cover some ground when you leave Houston. One hugely popular getaway is the island city of Galveston, famed for its beaches and Victorian architecture. The sand and water may be dingy brown, but they're only an hour away. Touring the Bishop's Palace (1402 Broadway, T 409 762 2475) gives a sense of Galveston's former grandeur, and the stately Hotel Galvez (2024 Seawall Boulevard, T 409 765 7721) lends a holiday feel. A few hours' drive east of Houston is Orange, on the Louisiana border, which enjoyed its own Victorian boom fuelled by East Texas timber. The Stark family of lumber barons left behind the Stark Museum of Art (712 Green Avenue, T 409 886 2787), which focuses on works from the American West, and the marble-and-granite First Presbyterian Church (902 Green Avenue, T 409 883 2097), one of the first air-conditioned buildings in the country when it opened in 1912. Another of the family's legacies is Shangri La (see p098), the botanical fantasy of scion HJ Lutcher Stark, now restored to its original splendour.

For a sense of how vast the state is, head west, past the urban sprawl and into the wide-open spaces. Here you can see Big Bend National Park (www.nps.gov/bibe), land art in towns like Marfa, home of the Judd Foundation (104 Highland Avenue, T 432 729 4406), and the spectacle of some of the world's largest wind farms. *For full addresses, see Resources.*

Cadillac Ranch, Amarillo

Texas has an abundance of land, artists and money, so it's little wonder that land art has flourished here, particularly in West Texas and the Panhandle, where the endless horizon is a perfect backdrop for installations such as the 1974 Cadillac Ranch, patronised by the helium tycoon Stanley Marsh 3. Turn up with spray paint; you're expected to leave your mark on the 10 Caddies half-buried outside Amarillo by San Francisco art collective Ant Farm. Then take in some of the region's other installations, such as Robert Smithson's 1973 Amarillo Ramp (T 806 584 2264) and Walter De Maria's 1977 Lightning Field (T 505 898 3335), which comprises 400 stainless-steel poles in the New Mexico desert and is open for overnight visits between May and October.
Interstate 40 between exits 60 and 62

JACOB-PAUL A STAR WARS BAR MITZVAH

Shangri La Botanical Gardens, Orange
Inspired by James Hilton's 1933 book *Lost Horizon*, HJ Lutcher Stark began building his own Eden in his hometown of Orange, 177km east of Houston, in 1937. Shangri La featured large azalea gardens situated alongside a cypress swamp – a beautiful setting that attracted thousands of visitors. The gardens were closed in 1958 following a snowstorm that killed most of the plants, but reopened in 2008 after a restoration funded by the Starks' foundation. Today, the 102-hectare reserve is a draw once again, its landscaping enhanced by a series of pavilions designed by San Antonio architects Lake|Flato for use as visitor and education centres. A few minutes' drive from here, the WH Stark House (T 409 883 0871) gives a glimpse of old Texas money. *2111 W Park Avenue, T 409 670 9113, www.starkculturalvenues.org*

Los Poblanos, New Mexico

Albuquerque is a two-hour flight from Houston, but culturally and visually it's a world away. Founded by the Spanish in 1706, the city has preserved much of its heritage, and Los Poblanos is an excellent place to experience this. The complex dates to 1932, when architect John Gaw Meem and regional artists converted a ranch into a cultural centre and a model farm. The Californian firm Moule & Polyzoides overhauled the site in 2011, creating 20 guest rooms with features like wood-burning fireplaces. All the requisite mod cons were installed too, but given the art and architecture tours, strolls through lavender fields and fine food on offer, the challenge may be finding the time to enjoy them. *4803 Rio Grande Boulevard NW, T 505 344 9297, www.lospoblanos.com*

Rocket Park
Bypass the touristy visitor complex at
the Johnson Space Center for this rather
nonchalant display of vintage space
vessels. Outside are early 1960s rockets,
but the highlight is the restored Saturn
V (pictured), the kind that took men to
the moon. Admission is free; tell the JSC
guard you're there to see Rocket Park.
*2nd Street at Saturn Lane,
Johnson Space Center, T 281 244 2100*

NOTES

SKETCHES AND MEMOS

RESOURCES

CITY GUIDE DIRECTORY

HOTELS

ADDRESSES AND ROOM RATES

Hotel Derek 016
Room rates:
double, $375
2525 W Loop South
T 713 961 3000
www.hotelderek.com

Hotel Galvez 096
Room rates:
double, from $140
2024 Seawall Boulevard
Galveston
T 409 765 7721
www.galveston.com/galvez

Hotel Icon 020
Room rates:
double, from $190;
Suite 1215, from $500;
Penthouse Suite, from $3,700
220 Main Street
T 713 224 4266
www.hotelicon.com

Modern B&B 022
Room rates:
double, $115;
Treehouse, $235
4003 Hazard Street
T 832 279 6367
www.modernbb.com

Los Poblanos 100
Room rates:
double, from $165
4803 Rio Grande Boulevard NW
Albuquerque
New Mexico
T 505 344 9297
www.lospoblanos.com

The Sam Houston Hotel 016
Room rates:
double, from $135
1117 Prairie Street
T 832 200 8800
www.thesamhoustonhotel.com

Hotel Sorella 017
Room rates:
double, from $170;
Junior Suite, from $270;
Penthouse, from $550
800 Sorella Court
T 713 973 1600
www.hotelsorella-citycentre.com

Hotel ZaZa 021
Room rates:
double, from $285;
Magnificent Seven Suite, from $1,500;
Rock Star Suite, from $2,500
5701 Main Street
T 713 526 1991
www.hotelzaza.com